THEN & NOW

CHICAGO'S LOOP

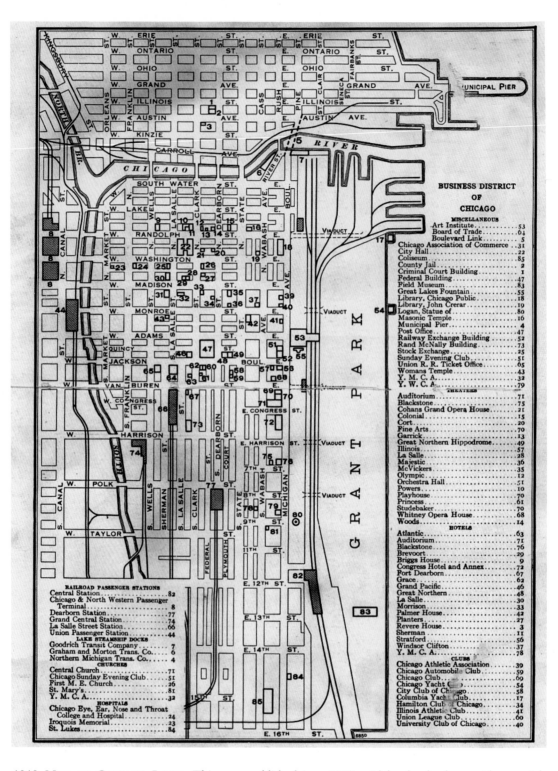

1919 MAP OF CHICAGO LOOP. This map, published in a 1919 guidebook, clearly provides a quick overview of Chicago, and documents that even back in 1919, Chicago was and continues to be a major metropolitan city. (Private Collection.)

THEN & NOW

CHICAGO'S LOOP

Janice A. Knox and Heather Olivia Belcher

ARCADIA

Published by Arcadia Publishing
Charleston SC, Chicago IL, Portsmouth NH, San Francisco CA

Printed in the United States of America

Library of Congress Catalog Card Number: 2002102521

For all general information contact Arcadia Publishing at:
Telephone 843-853-2070
Fax 843-853-0044
E-mail sales@arcadiapublishing.com
For customer service and orders:
Toll-Free 1-888-313-2665

Visit us on the Internet at http://www.arcadiapublishing.com

PANORAMIC VIEW OF CHICAGO LOOP AND LAKE MICHIGAN. This postcard view was taken east from the Majestic Building. Edmund R. Krause built the building, located at 22–22 West Monroe Street, in 1905. The 20-story building housed the Majestic Theatre, which is now known as the Schubert Theater. (Private Collection.)

Contents

Acknowledgments

STATE STREET NORTH FROM MADISON AVENUE, 1933. (Courtesy of the University of Illinois at Chicago.)

There are a number of people who provided support and encouragement during the production of this book, and much appreciation and gratitude goes out to these individuals. Patricia Bakunas, Zita Stukas, Carmen Deleon, and Mary Diaz, Special Collections Staff at the University of Illinois at Chicago, provided tremendous support in helping us to navigate and obtain permission to use the many historic photographs from the Chicago Photographic Collection. The full credit line for these photographs appears below. A special thanks goes out to Robert Sandla, Editor-in-Chief of Stagebill, who graciously allowed us to use advertisements from past Stagebill publications. Tom Yanul, photographer, provided great photographs of the opening day of the new financial futures floor at the Chicago Board of Trade. Samantha Gleisten and Julia Knippen, Arcadia Publishing, provided ongoing encouragement and support. Attorneys James Montgomery and Len Rubin should also be noted for their encouragement and guidance. We are also grateful to our friend, Patricia Robinson, who continues to keep us in her prayers and has provided encouragement, support, and friendship. Lastly, we are dedicating this book to our parents/grandparents, Lucy Olivia Knox and James W. Knox for their understanding, love, and encouragement, and to Betty J. Rutherford, sister and aunt, who is now in heaven, but her love of family and her laughter will always remain with us.

Special Note from Janice A. Knox: Much appreciation and love goes out to my daughter, the co-author Heather Olivia Belcher, who gave up many of her weekends and free time to photograph all of the contemporary views (except for the CBOT photograph noted above), and for being a good friend.

Note: Images from Chicago Photographic Collection, Department of Special Collections, The University Library, University of Illinois at Chicago.

Introduction

ELEVATED R.R. LOOP, VAN BUREN
STREET, CHICAGO.

A nostalgic look at the evolution of Chicago's Loop can only be accomplished by comparing historic photographs and postcards that document the beauty, elegance, and splendor of years past to the contemporary views of today. These images tell a powerful tale. From the introduction of cable cars that converged in the central business district in 1882 creating a "Loop" to the completion of the Union Elevated Loop Transit Lines in 1897, built almost entirely over the same path of the cable cars, the Chicago Loop has become a symbol to both visitors and residents alike. The two miles of elevated tracks help to define the 72-block rectangular-shaped area, which is often referred to as "Downtown."

Chicago was incorporated as a city on March 4, 1837, with a population of less than 5,000 and has grown to nearly three million people today. However, the origins of the business district goes back to Chicago's first settler, Jean Baptiste Point DuSable, a black fur trader who, with his Potowatomi Indian wife, established a very successful trading post on the north bank of the Chicago River. The celebration of the rich cultural diversity of Chicago began at that point and continues today.

The rapid growth of Chicago into a world-class financial and urban metropolitan center has not been without challenges. The Chicago Fire of 1871 nearly destroyed the city. Four square miles including the business district burned, but even before the embers had cooled, the city began to rebuild. The unofficial motto of Chicago, "I Will," is a testament of Chicago's will to survive.

The dedication and faith in the city is demonstrated by the previous generations who have built and rebuilt the Chicago Loop. The former social, racial, and gender boundaries of yesterday no longer exist. The urban planners have gracefully blended new architecture along with the old, resulting in a distinctive skyline, a beautiful park and lakefront, financial, retail, and theater districts that maintain the Chicago Loop as a world-class area that has something to offer everyone. Some of the historic structures no longer exist except in the images provided by those dedicated photographers of a bygone era. The Chicago Loop has recently been, and continues to be, revitalized. From the historic buildings going through extraordinary residential conversions, to the rebuilding of the Peristyle, from the Millennium Park plans to make a great park even better, to the development ideas for the land surrounding the Loop, these transformations have made Chicago "Our Kind of Town."

DOUBLE-DECKER BUSES ALONG MICHIGAN AVE, 1937. In 1917, the Chicago Motor Bus Co. began operating open-top, double-decker buses on many of the city's boulevards. (Courtesy of the University of Illinois at Chicago.)

SOLDIER FIELD, 1929. This aerial photo of Soldier Field and the Field Museum was taken in 1929 with the skyline of the Chicago Loop and Grant Park in the background. Were it not for the actions of retailer and property-owner, Aaron Montgomery Ward, the city of Chicago would not be able to maintain the open park space of Grant Park (formerly known as Lake Park prior to 1901). Soldier Field is home to the Chicago Bears (football) and the Chicago Fire (soccer) teams. The 100-foot Doric columns with tetra style temples give Soldier Field the look of a coliseum in Ancient Rome. Built in 1924 by Holabird and Roche, the field was originally called the Grant Park Stadium, but was later renamed to honor the fallen World War I soldiers. Originally built as a U-shaped structure as seen below, the stadium's northern end was closed in during the construction of the Chicago Park District Administrative Building, completed in

Chapter 1

CHICAGO'S FRONT YARD

1939. This building was demolished in 2001 in preparation for the controversial plan to renovate Soldier Field by building a new stadium within and above the outer façade of the current field, changes which may threaten its National Historic Landmark status. (Courtesy of the University of Illinois at Chicago.)

CHICAGO SKYLINE, *C.* **1940 & 2002.** The famous Chicago skyline has retained its distinctive look over the years, gracefully blending old and new architecture. (Postcard Private Collection, Photo by Heather Olivia Belcher.)

CLARENCE BUCKINGHAM FOUNTAIN, 1955 & 2002. The fountain is one of the many symbols of Chicago, and is located in Grant Park at Congress Street. Kate Buckingham (1858–1937) donated the fountain in 1927 as a $750,000 gift to the city of Chicago in memory of her brother, Clarence Buckingham (1854–1913), a former director of the Art Institute of Chicago. The fountain, modeled after the Latonia Fountain in the garden of Versailles in France, was built by Bennett, Parsons, and Frost from Chicago, and Marcel Francois Loyau and Jacques Lambert from Paris. One-and-a-half million gallons of water are re-circulated through 133 jets, at approximately 14,000 gallons a minute. During summer nights, a spectacular color light show is performed. Originally, the fountain was operated manually, but is now computer operated. In 1994, there was a restoration of the fountain, and it continues to be a favorite place to visit. (1955 Photo Courtesy of the University of Illinois at Chicago, 2002 Photo by Heather Olivia Belcher.)

MUNICIPAL PIER EXCURSION BOATS, *c.* 1920, NAVY PIER EXCURSION BOATS, 2002. In the 1920s, the cost of boat rides from the pier to Lincoln Park was a mere 25¢. Today, the cost is around $40, including lunch. Boats could also be taken from the pier to Jackson Park on the south side. The pier, which Charles S. Frost completed in 1916, was similar to the one that Burnham had planned in his 1909 Plan of Chicago. However, the pier in Burnham's Plan would have been constructed in Grant Park. (Postcard Private Collection, Photo by Heather Olivia Belcher.)

NAVY PIER, 1939 & 2002. One of the favorite places to visit in Chicago, Navy Pier was built as Municipal Pier No. 2 in 1916. Pier No. 1 was never built. Located at 600 East Grand Avenue at the lakefront, the 3,000-foot-long pier was built to provide ships with docking facilities for freight vessels and excursion steamers, warehouses, and public recreational facilities. At the time it was built, it was considered the world's longest pier. Due to the Great Depression and increased trans-portation advances, its usefulness started to decline. The U.S. Navy converted the pier to a training facility and changed the name to Navy Pier. The University of Illinois purchased the pier in 1946 to use as their Chicago Branch. In 1989, the City of Chicago established the Metropolitan Pier & Exposition Authority to oversee the renovation of the pier to be used as a recreational and cultural center. A 150-foot Ferris wheel, shops, theaters, museum, restaurants, and more continue to attract visitors year-round. (Postcard Private Collection, Photo by Heather Olivia Belcher.)

GRANT PARK, NORTH FROM THE FIELD MUSEUM, 1948 & 2002. The famous Chicago skyline has changed and in Grant Park, the Petrillo Band Shell has been relocated. The Clarence Buckingham Fountain can be seen in the 1948 view and still exists, but due to the angle of the 2002 shot, it's difficult to see the fountain and the bandshell through the trees. On July 1, 1935, free Grant Park concerts began under the guidance and support of James Petrillo, Commissioner of the Chicago Park District (1934-45) and President of the Chicago Federation of Musicians (1922-62). In 1975, the bandshell was renamed and dedicated to Petrillo. In 1978, a new music shell was built three-quarters of a mile north of the original bandshell. In 2003, another move is scheduled to a state-of-the-art music pavilion, designed by Frank Gehry as part of the Chicago Millennium Park. (1948 Photo Courtesy of the University of Illinois at Chicago, 2002 Photo by Heather Olivia Belcher.)

PETRILLO BAND SHELL, C. 1941 & 2002. During the great Depression, in 1931, Mayor Anton J. Cermak wanted to offer free concerts to "lift the spirits of Chicagoans." James C. Petrillo, President of the Chicago Federation of Musicians worked diligently to implement a series of free concerts in Grant Part to make classical music available to all Chicagoans and to provide employment for union musicians. On July 1, 1935, the Grant Park Concerts began with a march from Wagner's *Tannhauser.* The bandshell is still the home to the Grant Park Music Festival. Over the years, NBC and CBS provided broadcasts for the concerts, and some of the biggest stars of that period performed. In 2003, the Grant Music Festival will relocate to the new Millennium Park Music Pavilion, designed by Frank Gehry. (Postcard Private Collection, Photo by Heather Olivia Belcher.)

NORTH MICHIGAN AVENUE, MILLENNIUM PARK, *C.* **1920 & 2002.** This breathtaking view shows the dramatic skyline change along Michigan Avenue. The Grant Park renovation project, Millennium Park, includes the opening of an ice-skating rink and the rebuilding of the Peristyle Colonnade (built in 1917, and demolished in 1953) at Randolph Street. (1920 Photo Courtesy of the University of Illinois at Chicago, 2002 Photo by Heather Olivia Belcher.)

MICHIGAN BOULEVARD AND GRANT PARK LOOKING SOUTH FROM RANDOLPH STREET, 1929. On the bottom left of this view along Michigan Avenue shows, the semi-array of Greek columns known as the Peristyle can be seen. Built in 1917 by Chicago architect and city-planner, Edward H. Bennett, the concrete colonnade was demolished in 1953 in preparation for the construction of the Grant Park Underground Parking Garage. On the right, the Chicago Public Library (now Cultural Center, built in 1897), the People's Trust and Savings Building (now Illinois Federal Savings), Montgomery Ward Tower Building (1899), University Club (1909), Monroe Building (1912), Illinois Athletic Club (1908), People's Gas Building (1911), Railway Exchange (1904), New Straus building (1924), Auditorium (1889), Congress Hotel (1892), Harvester Building (1927), and the Blackstone Hotel (1909). The Art Institute (1892) is the only building seen in the distance in Grant Park. (Photo at right Courtesy of the University of Illinois at Chicago.)

MICHIGAN BOULEVARD AND GRANT PARK SOUTH FROM RANDOLPH STREET—MILLENNIUM PARK, 2002. The buildings along the west side of Michigan Avenue have largely remained intact. Part of the Millennium Park renovation project in Grant Park on the southwest corner includes a new parking garage, ice-skating ring, and a $5 million reconstruction of the Peristyle. Twelve pairs of 36-foot limestone, instead of concrete, columns are being constructed over a circular reflecting pool. Work should be completed by 2003. (Photos by Heather Olivia Belcher.)

MICHIGAN AVENUE AT JACKSON STREET LOOKING NORTH, 1950 & 2001. From the Railway Exchange Building (renamed Santa Fe Center, built in 1904 by D.H. Burnham) on the left at Jackson Street, the view down Michigan Avenue has changed. The Art Institute on the right in Grant Park still remains, but the commercial signage at Randolph Street—Coca-Cola and Pabst Blue Ribbon Beer—has been replaced by 39-story Doral Michigan Plaza (built in 1982 by Martin Reinnheimer); 40-story One Illinois Center (built in 1970 by the Office of Mies van der Rohe); 40-story One Prudential Plaza (built in 1955 by Naess & Murphy); 64-story Two Prudential Plaza (built in 1990 by Loebl, Schlossman & Hackl); and 82-story Amoco Building (built in 1973 by Edward Durell Stone, formerly known as the Standard Oil Building). The barriers and fences placed along Michigan Avenue in the photo on the left is part of the renovation for the Grant Park South Underground Parking Garage. (1950 Photo Courtesy of the University of Illinois at Chicago, 2001 Photo by Heather Olivia Belcher.)

CONGRESS PLAZA, 1945 & 2002.
This area serves as the grand entrance to Grant Park. The 17-foot equestrian statues, The Bowman and The Spearman, built in honor of Native Americans *c.*1928, and the entry pillars still exist today. However, the plaza and staircase were removed in 1955 for the extension of Congress Parkway into Grant Park. Additional restoration was done in 1994–95 to bring back the luster of the past. (1945 Photo Courtesy of the University of Illinois at Chicago, 2002 Photo by Heather Olivia Belcher.)

Illinois Central Depot, Chicago, Ill.

ILLINOIS CENTRAL STATION/PARK ROW, c. 1910 & 2002. Bradford L. Gilbert built the Illinois Central Station, located at South Michigan Avenue and Twelfth Street, in 1892 for about one million dollars. This station, also known as the Twelfth Street Station, was 7-stories high and had an impressive clock tower. The station marked the northern entrance to the 1933–34 Century of Progress World's Fair. The station was demolished in 1974, but trains continue to stop near this site. This postcard view shows the remaining residences of Park Row at the south end of Lake Front Park (now Grant Park), a fashionable area that once stood on this site. South of the train station stood the Hotel Imperial, a 300-room, 7-story hotel, built in 1891 at a cost of $200,000. Today, this area is being developed as luxury townhouses and high rises. (Postcard Private Collection, Photo by Heather Olivia Belcher.)

STATE AND RANDOLPH, 1946. The photograph, taken in 1946, shows a busy intersection that continues to be one of the shopping meccas of the Chicago Loop. On the northeast corner of State and Randolph Streets, Marshall Field's and Co., with its famous clock, has been a favorite meeting place for Loop shoppers and visitors. (Photo Courtesy of the University of Illinois at Chicago.)

Chapter 2

THE RETAIL
& FINANCIAL
DISTRICT
GROWS

MARSHALL FIELD'S & CO., c. 1906, AND 2002. "Give the lady what she wants," a motto attributed to Marshall Field, still symbolizes the famous department store's commitment to customer service. The store began on its current site in 1868, as Field & Leiter, but actually dates back to 1852 when Potter Palmer opened a small dry goods store on Lake Street. In 1868, Palmer built a "dry goods palace" at the cost of $350,000 on State and Washington and sold the business to Field & Leiter. The building lasted until the Chicago Fire of 1871. Several days after the fire, the store reopened at a temporary site outside of the fire-damaged area. Two subsequent buildings were constructed on this site: 1873–1877 and 1878–1905. The partnership lasted until 1882, and the business became Marshall Field's & Co. The postcard view above (c. 1906), shows the northern section, which had been completed in 1902 by D.H. Burnham. The southern section was completed in 1907, by D. H. Burnham & Co., as seen in the photo at the left. The northern section replaced the Central Music Hall, built in 1879 and demolished in 1901. Additions were made on the Wabash side. (Postcard Private Collection, Photo by Heather Olivia Belcher.)

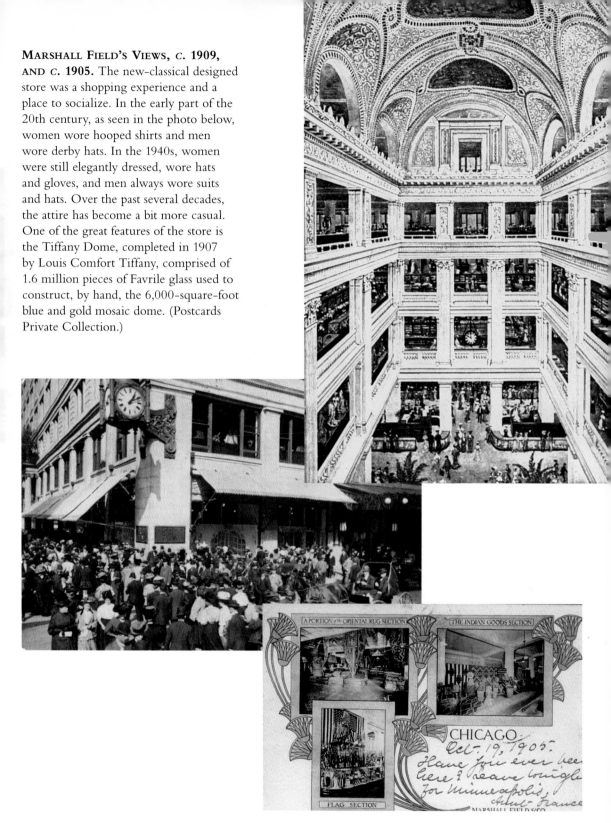

MARSHALL FIELD'S VIEWS, C. 1909, AND C. 1905. The new-classical designed store was a shopping experience and a place to socialize. In the early part of the 20th century, as seen in the photo below, women wore hooped shirts and men wore derby hats. In the 1940s, women were still elegantly dressed, wore hats and gloves, and men always wore suits and hats. Over the past several decades, the attire has become a bit more casual. One of the great features of the store is the Tiffany Dome, completed in 1907 by Louis Comfort Tiffany, comprised of 1.6 million pieces of Favrile glass used to construct, by hand, the 6,000-square-foot blue and gold mosaic dome. (Postcards Private Collection.)

SOUTHEAST CORNER STATE AND RANDOLPH,
c. **1941 & 2002**. This corner has not changed
much over the years. In 1941, at the Chicago
Theater, 175 North State Street, moviegoers of
that era were treated to live stage shows and a
movie. The Chicago Theater, a movie palace,
was built in 1921. Stage shows were discontinued
in the 1950s, and the movie theater closed in
1985 due to declining movie attendance. The
theater was renovated once for the 1933
World's Fair and again in 1986. After
the last extensive restoration in 1986, it
reopened for live shows and concerts.
Back in 1941, the small theater to the
right of the Chicago Theater, Telenews,
showed newsreels. It has since been
replaced by a store. The Masonic Temple
(or Capital Building) once stood on the
corner where Walgreens stands today. The
building, constructed in 1892 and demolished in 1939, was 21-stories and considered the tallest building in the world in
1892. The Walgreens drug store chain,
which started in 1901 with one store, has
over 3,700 stores. In the left background
of both photographs stands the Pure Oil
Building located at 35 East Wacker and
built in 1926. (1941 Photo Courtesy of
the University of Illinois at Chicago, 2002
Photo by Heather Olivia Belcher.)

STATE—MADISON BUILDING, C. 1952. The photo (right) taken from the Loop's busiest corner, the intersection of State and Madison Streets, is the center of Chicago's street numbering system. On the northwest corner, this half-block, 17-story commercial building is used for multiple occupants and dates back to 1905 when it was built by Holabird & Roche as the Boston Store, a department store chain. At one time, this store was considered the world's tallest building dedicated to a single business. By 1948, the Boston Store had liquidated its merchandise and changed its name to the State-Madison Building. Later it was renamed the 1 North Dearborn Street Building, in which First National Bank of Chicago rented a few floors. On the east side of the street is the Marshall Field's & Co. Store and on the southeast corner stands the Columbus Memorial Building (page 92), built in 1893 by W. W. Boyington and demolished in 1959. The commercial building once housed a number of physicians and dentists. (Photo Courtesy of the University of Illinois at Chicago.)

SEARS ROEBUCK & COMPANY, 2002. The Sears flagship store (left) returned to the Chicago Loop on May 23, 2001, after an 18-year absence and now occupies the State-Madison Building. The department store chain has leased the lower 5-stories (a 250,000-square-foot space) and has made changes to return the building to department store use. The familiar clock has been removed and extensive renovation has taken place, but the historic building still retains its grandeur of years past. Although the Roosevelt Theater is gone, the Chicago Theater and the Marshall Field's & Co. flagship store remains as seen in both photographs. The streetlights have changed over the years and the new replacement lights along State Street look identical to the ones of the past. On the southeast corner of Washington and State Streets, across from Marshall Field's, is the 3-story Old Navy clothing store, which now occupies the spot where the Columbus Memorial Building once stood. (Photo by Heather Olivia Belcher.)

CARSON, PIRIE, SCOTT & CO., C. 1900 & 2002. This landmark, built from 1898 to 1906, with additions added in 1960–61, is located at 1 South State Street, at the southeast corner of Madison and State. Samuel Carson, John T. Pirie, and George and Robert Scott purchased the store in 1904. Carson and Pirie were actually related to each other, each having married the other's sister. Louis Sullivan designed the initial store including the ornate filigree cast-ironwork entrance. He cleverly included his initials into the entrance designs. Before acquiring the Schlessinger & Mayer Store, Carson's was located in the Reliance Building, one block north on State Street. Daniel H. Burnham & Co. made the 1906 additions, and the 1960–61 additions were completed by Holabird & Root. Extensive exterior renovations by John Vinci were made in 1979–80. In 1989, P.A. Bergner Co. of Milwaukee purchased Carson's. Since 1998, Saks Incorporated has been the owner. Carson's Christmas window displays continue to be a popular place to visit. The Schlesinger & Mayer building (built in 1872), DeJonghe's Hotel, and the Windsor-Clifton Hotel, previously occupied this site. (Postcard Private Collection, Photo by Heather Olivia Belcher.)

STATE AND MADISON, LOOKING EAST, *C.* 1907 & 2002. In 1900, architects Holabird & Roche built Mandel Bros. department store on the right at the northeast corner. The Wabash addition was built in 1905. The McClurg Building and the 1–3 North State Street Building, both built in 1872, formerly stood on the Mandel Bros. site. On the southeast corner is the Carson Pirie Scott & Co. department store built from 1899 to 1906, with additions added in 1927 and again in 1961. The Schlesinger & Mayer Building (built in 1872), the DeJonghe's, and the Windsor Clifton Hotels formerly occupied the Carson's site. On the east side of the elevated tracks on Michigan Avenue stands the Montgomery Ward & Co. Building, built in 1899. Mandel Bros. became the Wieboldt's Store and now several retail stores and offices are housed in the former department store. Carson Pirie Scott remains a department store today. The Montgomery Ward Building was renamed the 6 North Michigan Avenue building, and it is now being converted to condominium apartments. (Postcard Private Collection, Photo by Heather Olivia Belcher.)

NORTH AMERICAN BUILDING, 1933 & 1940, STATE STREET SOUTH FROM MADISON. Holabird & Roche built the North American Building, located at 36 South State Street, in 1912. The majority of the buildings along the street have changed since 1940. The 19-story building housed office and retail stores. A building housing the music store, Lyon & Healy, and the Royal Palm Building previously occupied this site. (Photos Courtesy of the University of Illinois at Chicago.)

NORTH AMERICAN BUILDING. A fashionable, buffet-style restaurant opened in 1891 on the northwest corner of State and Monroe Streets in the North American Building. The American Building remains vacant today, but there has been some speculation that it will be converted to a hotel or condominium complex. A large toy store has replaced some of the buildings. (Postcard Private Collection, 2002 photo by Heather Olivia Belcher.)

THIS SPACE FOR WRITING

POST CARD

PLACE STAMP HERE

The North American Restaurant
Northwest Corner State and Monroe Sts.
[ESTABLISHED 1891]

Chicago's Most Unusual Dining Place

Because you "serve yourself" and get big portions of the finest quality food at prices 'way below those charged elsewhere.

Because it is unique among general restaurants in that it also specializes in fish and sea-foods at prices within the reach of all.

Because it has broken all restaurant records—nearly two million people having dined here the past year.

Open from 7 a.m. until Midnight. Sundays and Holidays, too

C. O. KROPF CO., MILWAUKEE

the store's motto, "Everything for Everybody." In the 1920s, the Fair Store had its own radio station, but eventually this station was taken over by the Chicago Daily News. In 1965, the Fair Store was remodeled and became the downtown store of Montgomery Ward and Company. The building was demolished, and the site remained vacant, until construction began recently for the Dearborn Center, a new office complex. (1930 Photo Courtesy of the University of Illinois at Chicago, 2002 Photo by Heather Olivia Belcher.)

THE FAIR DEPARTMENT STORE, C. 1930, DEARBORN CENTER, 2002.
One of Chicago's most famous department stores, the second Fair Store, was built in 1891 and occupied a full block along Adams Street, between Dearborn and State Streets. The 11-story building, designed by William LeBaron Jenney (1832–1907), who was the inventor of "steel frame" architecture, had 19 acres, or 810,500 square feet, of selling space. The original store, built in 1875, was much smaller, having only 1,280 square feet of selling space. The founder, Ernest J. Lehman, provided affordable items to his customers that demonstrated

**DAVIS STORE, 1929, DEPAUL
CENTER, 2002.** The Davis Store,
owned by Marshall Field's, located on
the northeast corner of South State
and East Van Buren Streets, was built
in 1912 by Holabird & Roche. The
Davis Store remained at this site until
1936. The 10-story building also
housed the Goldblatt Store until 1981.
In 1991, DePaul University converted
the building for university, retail, and
professional use, and included space
for a food court. The building went
through renovation in 1993. The store
was originally the Rothschild Store
until, in 1923, Rothschild relocated
to the building across the street, at the
southwest corner of State and Jackson.
The site was previously occupied by
a Rothschild Store, built in 1894 by
Holabird & Roche and demolished
around 1910. The distinctive "R"
logo remains between each arch on
the lower level of the building as
seen in the photo below. (1929 Photo
Courtesy of the University of Illinois
at Chicago, 2002 Photo by Heather
Olivia Belcher.)

STATE AND JACKSON, LYTTON BUILDING, WALGREENS, GOLDBLATT, C. 1940 & 2002.

In the center of the above photo, the Lytton Building stands on the northeast corner of State and Jackson. Marshall & Fox built this 19-story building, home to a long-time retail store on State Street, in 1913. Today, the building is known as the 14 East Jackson Parkway Building and continues to house retail stores and offices. The Lytton store has gone out of business. Across the street, at the southeast corner, stands Walgreens Drug Store, also identified with Chicago. Walgreens has since moved across the street to the southwest corner occupying the old Rothschild Store. The site where Walgreens once stood on the southeast corner is a small plaza used as a northern entranceway to the DePaul Center (once known as Goldblatt Bros., Davis, and Rothschild Store). The Goldblatt's Store closed in 1982, soon after the opening of the Street Mall in 1979. (1940 Photo Courtesy of the University of Illinois at Chicago, 2002 Photos by Heather Olivia Belcher.)

RANDOLPH AND STATE, NW CORNER—STATE-RANDOLPH BUILDING, BUTLER BUILDING, AND STATE-LAKE THEATER, 1950 & 2002. Located on the northwest corner of State and Randolph, several office and retail buildings illustrated the variety of businesses and services available in the Loop area. On the corner, the 7-story State-Randolph Building, formerly known as the Dyche Building, was built in 1873 and demolished in 1955. Several doors down at 162 North State is the 16-story Butler Building, built in 1924 by architect C.A. Eckstorm. The building was renamed the Illinois Medical Training Center Building. Next to the Butler, at 190 North State, is the 12-story State-Lake Building built in 1917 by architects Rapp & Rapp. The building housed a 2,800-seat theater,

which opened as a vaudeville theater and become one of the RKO movie chain theaters. In the 1980s, the theater closed and the building was renamed the ABC/WLS building. The State-Lake name remains over the front entrance. A new office building replaced the Randolph-State Building and Border's Bookstore occupies the lower floors. (1950 Photo Courtesy of the University of Illinois at Chicago, 2002 Photo by Heather Olivia Belcher.)

FEDERAL RESERVE BANK, 1938 & 2002. The Federal Reserve Bank Building, at 230 South LaSalle Street, stands on the northwest corner of LaSalle and Jackson. Graham, Anderson, Probst & White built the 14-story building in 1922. In 1957, Naess & Murphy completed a southwest addition. Holabird & Root completed a northwest addition in 1989. Buildings previously occupying this site were as follows: Royal Insurance (built in 1885, demolished in 1920); Medinah (1893-1969); Wells-Quincy (1914-1959); 230 South Wells (1886/1950-1990); Mallers (1884-1920); and Gaff (1884-1920). Today, due to heightened security, concrete barriers have been placed around the building. Quincy Street, north of the building, has also been closed to traffic. (1938 Photo Courtesy University of Illinois at Chicago, 2002 Photo by Heather Olivia Belcher.)

THE CHICAGO BOARD OF TRADE (CBOT) BUILDING IN 1886. The building, as seen on the right in 1886, was built and dedicated on April 29, 1885. The 10-story construction, built with granite and a 300-foot clock tower, was located at LaSalle Street at Jackson Boulevard. The building, designed by William W. Boyington, was the first permanent home of the CBOT. The organization previously resided in numerous locations in the Chicago Business District.

The CBOT was founded in March 1848 to fill the need for a centralized grain market. The first home of the CBOT was in a room over the Gage and Haines Flour Store located at 101 South Water Street. The first meeting was held in March of 1848. The Exchange moved six times before relocating to rooms in the Chamber of Commerce Building at LaSalle and Washington Streets. The Rookery Building and the Royal Insurance Company are shown on the right and below. (Courtesy of the University of Illinois at Chicago.)

CBOT, c. 1890 & 2002. The CBOT Building seen in this postcard, c.1890s, after the dome of the clock tower had been removed.

On the far left, the 45-story CBOT was built in 1930 by Holabird & Root. There is a 32-foot tall aluminum statue of Ceres, the Roman Goddess of Grain. Since the statue was 309 feet above the street, the sculptor John Storrs assumed no one would be able to see the face of the statue, so he designed it without a face. An annex building to the Chicago Board of Trade was built in 1997. (Postcard Private Collection, 2002 Photo by Heather Olivia Belcher.)

CHICAGO BOARD OF TRADE IN 1913. The trading floor scene, often known as the "pit," was located in the old Chicago Board of Trade building constructed in 1883 and later demolished to make room for the current building constructed in 1930. Before child-labor laws were enacted, many young men worked on the trading

floor. This trading floor was located in the old Board of Trade Building, and it was the first commercial building constructed in Chicago that had electric lighting, some of which can be seen suspended from the ceiling in the photograph. (Courtesy of the University of Illinois at Chicago.)

CHICAGO BOARD OF TRADE—NEW TRADING FACILITY GRAND OPENING CEREMONY, 1997. On February 18, 1997, the $182 million trade facility opened as the world's largest. The 92,000-square-foot facility has been designed with state-of-the art technology to facilitate more efficient and quicker order processing for the CBOT. Attending the opening ceremony were former Illinois Governor Jim Thompson, Rep. Danny Davis, and Chicago Mayor Richard M. Daley among other civic and corporate leaders. (Photos Courtesy of Tom Yanul.)

Daniel H. Burnham built the First National Bank Building, pictured on the left, in 1903. The building was located at 38 South Dearborn, near the corner of Dearborn and Monroe Streets, on the site formerly occupied by the Montauk Building. Burnham's building was demolished in 1970. The First National Bank built a new, more modern facility at the opposite end of the block, on the site of the former Morrison Hotel. After the Bank relocated, the former building was razed and replaced by a two-level plaza, which included the 3,000-foot-long glass mural, *The Four Seasons,* designed by Marc Chagall and given as a gift to the City of Chicago. Today, the building is still home to a bank, but the business is now known as Bank One. (1955 Photo Courtesy of the University of Illinois at Chicago, 2001 Photo by Heather Olivia Belcher.)

FIRST NATIONAL BANK OF CHICAGO, 1955 & 2001. In 1863, the First National Bank opened its doors in the offices of Edmund Aiken, located at 22 LaSalle Street. In 1868, the bank constructed a fireproof building of iron, stone, and brick at State and Washington Streets. The great Chicago Fire of 1871 destroyed the "fireproof" building, but the bank safes, vaults, and their contents were saved in spite of the tremendous fire damage. The company moved back into the same location three months later.

CHICAGO LOOP, C. 1940. Looking north along LaSalle Street, this photograph was taken *c.*1940 from the top of the Chicago Board of Trade Building overlooking the center of the financial district. On the right stands the 45-story Morrison Hotel Tower, built in 1927 at 15-29 South Clark Street. The Morrison Hotel began as a 4-story structure in the late 1880s and later grew to 8 stories. A new hotel was built in 1913 with a 519-room capacity. Additional sections were added to the hotel in 1916 and 1925, increasing the hotel's capacity to 2,500. The tower replaced the 4-story section of the hotel. The hotel was demolished in 1966.

The Loop area once accommodated the residential needs of early Chicago. As more businesses and buildings were constructed, however, residents—especially those with financial means—tended to move out of the central business district. After the Chicago Fire, there was a great rebuilding effort, and displaced retail and commercial

Chapter 3

VISITORS & RESIDENTS
A Place to Stay

businesses soon began to make plans to return to the area destroyed by the fire. Luxury townhouses, for example, at Park Row near Twelfth Street, were still scattered around the fringes of the business district, but were soon replaced after the turn of the 20th century. (Photo Courtesy of the University of Illinois at Chicago.)

The Blackstone Hotel
presents in the

MAYFAIR ROO
JOAN EDWARDS
Your Favorite Hit Parade Star
JOE MERMAN and his orchestr

BALINESE ROO
BILL BENNETT'S TRIC

Dinner or Late Supper After The Theatre

The Blackstone
A Kirkeby Hotel

Avenue Building, part of Columbia College. (1941 Photo Courtesy of the University of Illinois at Chicago, 1948 Ad Courtesy of Stagebill, 2001 Photo by Heather Olivia Belcher.)

BLACKSTONE HOTEL, 1941 & 2001. Benjamin Marshall and Charles Fox built the Blackstone Hotel in 1909. The 500-room hotel was located on the northwest corner of Balbo and Michigan Avenue at 636 South Michigan. The Blackstone Hotel, also known as the Sheraton Blackstone, was closed in 1999. The 22-story structure was built based on the specifications of Timothy Blackstone, President of the Illinois Central Railroad, who wanted the hotel to be a home away from home for wealthy guests. In recognition of the hotel's excellence in design, the Illinois Chapter of the AIA awarded the hotel a gold medal in 1909. Two years later, in 1910, the Blackstone Theater was built adjacent to the hotel. In 1920, in Suite 408, Warren G. Harding was selected as the Republican nominee for President. Today, the hotel is being converted to condos. The site was formerly the home of Timothy Blackstone, President of the Chicago & Alton Railroad. Next to the Blackstone is the Blum Building, built in 1908 with additional floors added in 1922, also known as the Musical College, Barnheisel, Grant Park, Torco, and now the 624 South Michigan

STEVENS HOTEL, 1927, CONRAD HILTON HOTEL, 2002. The Stevens Hotel (now known as the Conrad Hilton), owned by Ernest J. Stevens, is located at 720 South Michigan Avenue at Balbo Street. It was built by Holabird and Roche and opened in May 1927. On the rooftop, there was an 18-hole miniature golf course, one of the many novelties the hotel offered. During the Depression in the 1930s, the hotel went bankrupt. During World War II, in 1943, the Stevens was used as an Army Air Corps military training facility. One year later, it reopened as a hotel. In 1951, the Stevens Hotel was renamed the Conrad Hilton, after the 1945 purchase by Conrad Hilton for $7.5 million. The hotel has 25 stories and a 4-story tower and was the largest hotel in the world when it was built. From 1984 through 1986, the firm of Solomon, Cordwell, and Buenz, restored the hotel to its former luster. This renovation reduced the number of rooms from 3,000 to 1,620, but increased their size and amenities. The 2-story Arcade Building was formerly built on this site. (1927 Photo Courtesy of the University of Illinois at Chicago, 2002 Photo by Heather Olivia Belcher.)

STEVENS HOTEL
AND MICHIGAN AVE.

KAUFMANN & FABRY

level in Grant Park and on the lakefront had to obtain the consent of all of the property owners on that portion of Michigan Avenue along Grant Park. The building also had a 390-foot tower with a 22 1/2-foot weather vane in the form of a female figure designed by J. Massey Rhine. Montgomery Ward sold the building in 1908, and the tower portion of the building was removed in 1947, as it was then considered unsafe. The weather vane was destroyed sometime during the tower removal. A similar weather vane sits on top of the current Montgomery Ward's Building on Chicago Avenue. The former building on Michigan Avenue continued to be used for retail and business, and is being renovated to provide additional luxury housing in the Loop area. The Montgomery Ward stores have recently gone out of business. (Postcard Private Collection, Photo by Heather Olivia Belcher.)

MONTGOMERY WARD & COMPANY BUILDING, C. 1908 & 2002. The Italian Renaissance skyscraper, also known as the Tower Building, was completed in 1899 by Richard E. Schmidt to serve as the Montgomery Ward & Company Headquarters. Aaron Montgomery Ward's 12-story office building, located at 6 North Michigan Avenue at the northwest corner of Madison Street and Michigan Avenue, was enhanced by the unobstructed view of Grant Park and Lake Michigan. He filed numerous lawsuits against others who planned on constructing buildings in Grant Park. The Illinois Supreme Court rulings helped to protect the beauty of Grant Park for many years to come; anyone wishing to construct a building above ground

**MICHIGAN AVENUE NORTH FROM
AUDITORIUM ANNEX (CONGRESS HOTEL,
1916 & 2002.)** The Congress Hotel was
originally built in 1893 by Clinton J. Warren
as a 10-story annex to the Auditorium
Building, and is located at 520 South
Michigan. The hotel opened in time to
accommodate visitors to the 1893 World's

Columbian Exposition. Holabird & Roche later added additions
in 1902 and 1907. The hotel also has a colorful political history. In
1912, former President Theodore Roosevelt hosted the Bull Moose
Convention at the Congress Hotel, causing a split in the Republican
Party. Although Roosevelt had won most of the party's primaries, the
incumbent William Howard Taft had control of the Republican Party.
The party supported Taft for re-election, so the Progressive Party was
formed to support Roosevelt. However, the Democratic candidate
Woodrow Wilson won the Presidential Election. In 1932, Franklin D.
Roosevelt accepted the Democratic presidential nomination at the
Congress Hotel. Michigan Avenue has changed over the years, but
there is a continual renovation of the majestic skyscrapers to blend
luxury residential housing with newer constructions. The Congress
Hotel has also been known as the American Congress, Pick-Congress,
Ramada Congress, and today, as the Congress Plaza Hotel. (Postcard
Private Collection, Photos by Heather Olivia Belcher.)

before it closed on February 2, 1973. The building was demolished in 1980 to make room for the State of Illinois Center, now known as the Thompson Center (below left). The access tunnel in the center of the street is now used as an ornamental planter. Tunnels were built for wagons and pedestrians to travel under the Chicago River. This tunnel was originally opened in 1870 and was used to escape the Great Fire in 1871. However, in 1906, Congress closed all underground tunnels, citing hazards to river navigation. Between 1910–12, the tunnels were renovated and subsequently reopened. (1940 Photo Courtesy of the University of Illinois at Chicago, Postcard Private Collection, 2002 Photo by Heather Olivia Belcher.)

HOTEL SHERMAN, C. 1940 & 2002. The Hotel Sherman first opened as the City Hotel in 1837, on the north side of Randolph between Clark and LaSalle. In 1844, it was renamed the Sherman House after its owner, Francis C. Sherman, who served three terms as the mayor of Chicago. The hotel was destroyed in the 1871 fire, but was quickly rebuilt by William W. Boyington, who also built the Water Tower and many other structures in Chicago. The Hotel Sherman was renovated several times

PALMER HOUSE, 1912 & 2002 There have been four Palmer House structures built in the Loop. The structure pictured below is the third building. The current and fourth 25-story, 2,000 room hotel, shown right, was designed by Holabird & Roche and was constructed between 1925–27. It is now part of the Hilton Hotel chain and has been renamed the Palmer House Hilton. The first hotel was on the northwest corner of State and Quincy on the site of the home of its architect, John M. Van Osdel. The second and fourth buildings were built on the same location, the southeast corner of State and Monroe. Building two opened in March of 1871, but was destroyed seven months later in the Chicago Fire. The architect's records had been stored in clay under the basement floor; the fire baked the clay, but the records remained intact and another method of fireproofing was discovered. The third 7-story Palmer House was designed by John M. Van Odell and built in 1875 at a cost of $2.5 million. This building remained until 1925 and was one of the earliest hotels to have electric lights, elevators, and telephones. The hotel claimed to be the world's first fireproof hotel. In 1879, the Grand Dining Room hosted a banquet for General Ulysses S. Grant and Mark Twain was the dinner speaker. (Photo Private Collection, Photo by Heather Olivia Belcher.)

YMCA HOTEL
822 S.WabashAv
CHICAGO
&
1800 Rooms
30 to 60 cents
per day

YMCA HOTEL, 1919, C. 1930, 2001. The 19-story YMCA Hotel, at 826 South Wabash Avenue, was built in 1915 by Robert C. Berlin. An addition, built at the same height on the south in 1926, was built by Berlin & Swern. In 1988, an 8-story addition was made and the building was converted to mixed uses including a multi-screen movie theater. It was renamed the Burnham Park Plaza Building. (Postcards Private Collection, Photo by Heather Olivia Belcher.)

ROOF GARDEN
YMCA HOTEL
CHICAGO, ILLINOIS

STATE AND WASHINGTON, 1928. Looking north along State Street from Washington Street in 1928, three of the finest downtown theaters are shown. Only the Chicago Theatre on the right, built in 1921, remains. On the left, the Roosevelt Theater, built in 1921 and demolished in 1990, is now a vacant lot fondly called "Block 37." The State-Lake Theatre Building, built in 1917, has been renamed the ABC/WLS Building. The theater is gone, but now converted for use by the television station. (Photo Courtesy of the University of Illinois at Chicago.)

Chapter 4
THE GOLDEN AGE OF ENTERTAINMENT & CULTURAL ACTIVITIES

CHICAGO OFFICE OF FRINK & WALKER'S STAGE LINES, 1850

ONE OF THE SIXTEEN HISTORICAL PAINTINGS BY LAWRENCE C. EARLE IN THE BANKING ROOM OF THE
CENTRAL TRUST COMPANY OF ILLINOIS 125 WEST MONROE ST., CHICAGO
· REAL ESTATE LOAN DEPT. & SAFE DEPOSIT VAULTS ·

FRINK, WALKER & CO. STAGECOACH OFFICE, 1850, GOODMAN THEATRE (HARRIS & SELWYN THEATRES), 2002. In 1837, Frink and Walker purchased the stagecoach office at the southwestern corner of Lake and Dearborn Streets. They had the first stage route between Chicago and Rockford, Illinois. The first run, on January 1, 1838, took 24 hours—one way! From 1873 to 1922, the Dickey Building stood at this location and was once the home of Northwestern University's Law School. In 1923, Howard Crane & Kenneth Franzheim built the 3-story Harris and Selwyn Theatres, which hosted plays and live theater. The overall decline of the theatre district eventually affected both venues. The theaters were renamed the Michael Todd and Cinestage Theaters, and later, the Dearborn Cinemas. Eventually, the landmark theaters closed and remained vacant for many years and were almost demolished, until the Goodman announced it would build a new, $46 million complex at that location. The theaters' terra cotta façades were preserved and incorporated into the new Goodman Theatre, which made a stunning complement to the new structure when the Goodman reopened on December 11, 2000. (Postcard Private Collection, Photos by Heather Olivia Belcher.)

50

CASTLE THEATER, 1928, TOYS "R" US/KIDS "R" US, 2002. In 1928, theater patrons flocked to the Castle Theater to see the film version of the Broadway hit *The Jazz Singer*, starring Al Jolson (in black face). The Castle Theater, located at 6 South State Street, was completed in 1915 and first opened on January 26, 1916. The theater seated 300 and was one of the many vaudeville theaters in the Loop. In the late-1920s, the Castle was remodeled and wired for sound. Clarence Beck, in 1932, converted the Castle into the first all-newsreel movie house in Chicago. Thirty-minute newsreel shows could be seen for a mere 15¢. Over the years, a number of retail businesses occupied the site. For the past decade, the Toys "R" Us/Kids "R" Us occupied a 60,000-square-foot store on the site, which included the Castle Theater. Due to plans by the retailer to scale back

their operation, this store will be closing in 2002, and a search is in progress to find another tenant to lease the store. (1928 Photo Courtesy University of the Illinois at Chicago, 2002 Photo by Heather Olivia Belcher.)

5025

FIELD MUSEUM OF NATURAL HISTORY, C. 1930 & 2002. The Field Museum of Natural History first opened in 1894 to house the natural history collections from the 1893 World's Columbian Exposition. Originally, it was called the Columbian Museum of Chicago. After the close of the fair, it opened at the Palace of Fine Arts in Jackson Park. The collection was relocated to Grant Park at Fourteenth Street upon completion of the new building in 1921 by D.H. Burnham & Co. When Marshall Field donated $9 million toward construction costs, the museum's name was changed in 1905. The 3-story building, made of white Georgia marble, was constructed on a landfill donated by the Illinois Central Railroad. The lines on opening day, May 2, 1921, were over a quarter-of-a-mile long. For the next 42 years, Stanley Field, Marshall Field's nephew, served as the unpaid president of the museum and subsequent Chairman of the Board. The museum is part of the Museum Campus Complex, along with the planetarium and aquarium. (Postcard Private Collection, Photos by Heather Olivia Belcher.)

JOHN G. SHEDD AQUARIUM, C. 1930, 2002. Located at 1200 South Lake Shore Drive, this structure was built on wood piles by Graham, Anderson, Probst, & White in 1929. The white marble building was modeled after the Field Museum, located nearby in the Museum Campus Complex. The Aquarium was named after the former president of Marshall Field & Company, Shedd, who had worked his way up from stock boy to President. He held that position from 1906 to 1923 and then became Chairman of the Board, which allowed him more time to devote to his civic activities. Shedd donated $3 million for the aquarium's construction. In 1991, expansion included the construction of the Oceanarium—a modern marine mammal pavilion—by Lohan Associates. The Aquarium is the largest public aquarium in the world. (Postcard Private Collection, Photo by Heather Olivia Belcher.)

ICAGO - JOHN G. SHEDD AQUARIUM

GREAT WHITE WAY, 1953 & 2002, AD OF CAFÉ DE ALEX (1932). Over the years, Randolph was been considered the entertainment and theater district of the Chicago Loop. At one time, there were at least nine major theaters along or near this street. A number of restaurants were also found along Randolph to appeal to a variety of tastes. When theater attendance began to decline, the venues first became third-rate movie houses and then closed and were eventually demolished. The Oriental Theater (now the Ford Center for Performing Arts), Goodman Theater (utilizing the restored Harris and Selwyn Theatres), Cadillac Palace Theater (formerly Bismarck and RKO Palace), and the newly open Noble Fool Theater have begun to bring back some of the sparkle to this street. There are also a number of restaurants returning to this area. (Postcard Private Collection, Ad Courtesy of Stagebill, Photo by Heather Olivia Belcher.)

Cafe de Alex

80 W. RANDOLPH ST.

AFTER THE THEATER

Tonight and Every Night—
Enjoy excellent Spanish and
French Cuisine in an atmosphere of Old Spain! Continuous All-Native Entertainment
7:30p.m. 'til Closing. Dance to
MARTI'S CASTILIANS

| Luncheon, Dinner Daily, also A La Carte-from 11 a. m. | TEA DANSANT Saturday Afternoon $1 per person |

No Cover Charge At Any Time

On Near North Side:
CASA de ALEX
58 E. DELAWARE PLACE

Management of DANIEL ALEXANDER

THE IROQUOIS THEATRE, C. 1906, ORIENTAL THEATRE, FORD CENTER FOR THE PERFORMING ARTS, 2002. The Iroquois Theatre, on Randolph between State and Dearborn, opened in November 1903. Architect Benjamin H. Marshall's design was influenced by the new Edwardian playhouses of London. The theater featured a massive foyer, sweeping stairways, and multicolored marble. It was thought to be a fireproof structure. Five weeks later, on Wednesday, December 30, 1903, during a performance of *Mr. Blue Beard*, a tragic fire killed 600 people, many of whom were children. Many died due to blocked exits and the panic and subsequent stampede of the audience. The disaster initiated new

fire protection laws regarding theaters. The structure was not seriously damaged, so in 1904, the Iroquois reopened as Hyde and Behman's Music Hall. The Iroquois sign on the front of the theater was covered up by the Vaudeville sign, as shown on the postcard below. In 1905, it reopened again as the Colonial. In 1924–25, the Colonial was demolished and replaced by the New United Masonic Temple and Oriental Theatre Building, built in 1926 by Cornelius W. and George L. Rapp, and later became the Ford Center for the Performing Arts. To the left of the Iroquois is the landmark Delaware Building. (Postcard Private Collection, Photos Courtesy Heather Olivia Belcher.)

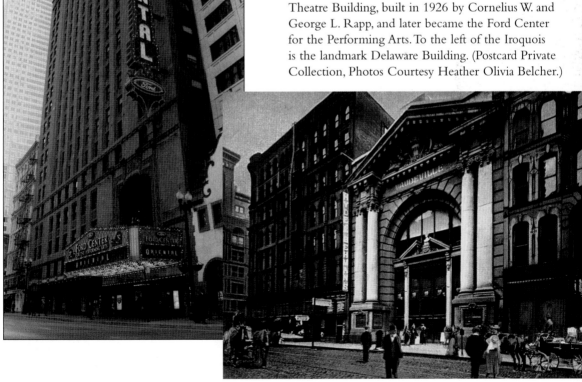

AUDITORIUM HOTEL AND ANNEX, c. 1917, 2002. Built in 1889, the 400-room Auditorium Hotel was located on the northwest corner of Congress Street and Michigan Avenue at 430 South Michigan Avenue. The hotel was part of the Auditorium complex, which included an office building and the 4,200-seat Auditorium Theatre. Designed by Dankmar Adler and Louis Sullivan, this 17-story building was the tallest building in America in 1889. The Auditorium Theatre, known for its well-equipped stage and perfect acoustics, featured 15 million pieces of colored marble in Sullivan's mosaic decorations. The Chicago Symphony Orchestra presented its inaugural concert on October 16, 1891, but moved to the Theodore Thomas Orchestra Hall in 1905. For many years, the Chicago Opera Company used the Auditorium, but in 1929, it moved to the new Civic Opera Building and the theater closed. From 1942–45, the hotel became the Chicago Servicemen's Center—USO. The theater was converted into a recreation hall, and the stage became bowling alleys. Roosevelt College purchased the hotel after the war in 1946 and it still exists today as Roosevelt University. The Auditorium Theatre stayed closed for 26 years and reopened on October 31, 1967. (Postcard Private Collection, Photo by Heather Olivia Belcher.)

AUDITORIUM INTERIOR VIEW POSTCARDS, 1907 & 1905. This artistic view of the auditorium and surrounding buildings is postmarked July 17, 1907. Alvion sent a series of interior view cards on November 25, 1905 to Miss. Mae L. Burns, Brokaw Hospital in Bloomington, Illinois. (Postcard Private Collection.)

AUDITORIUM AND ANNEX, CHICAGO.

ANNEX OFFICE

AUDITORIUM AND ANNEX, CHICAGO.

TIFFANY FOUNTAIN—POMPEIIAN ROOM.

AUDITORIUM THEATRE PLAYBILL. *Hellz a Poppin* starred Billy House and Eddie Garr. (Ad courtesy of Stagebill.)

1879, as the Chicago Academy of Fine Arts. It was renamed the Art Institute on December 21, 1882. The second home was on the southwest corner of Michigan and Van Buren Street, built in 1887 by Burnham & Root. (Postcards Private Collection, Photo by Heather Olivia Belcher.)

The Art Institute of Chicago · Michigan Avenue at Adams S

ART INSTITUTE OF CHICAGO, C. 1905 & 2002. The Art Institute of Chicago, pictured above and below in the vintage postcards and in the photograph on the right, is the third home of this institution. Located on South Michigan Avenue in Grant Park at Adams Street, this building was completed in 1893 by Shepley, Rutan & Coolidge in preparation for the 1893 World's Columbian Exposition. The World's Congress Auxiliary of the Exposition first used the building, and it was then dedicated on December 8, 1893. Over the years, a number of additions were made to house the expanding collections, but the original design has been maintained on Michigan Avenue, while the additions are located toward the rear of the structure. A pair of bronze lions guard the entrance and were designed by Edward L. Kemeys. The Art Institute was incorporated on May 24,

Art Institute. Chicago

You must come to see this. Its fine. Grace.

No. 280   Published by The Western News Company, Chicago, Berlin and Leipzig

58

THEODORE THOMAS ORCHESTRA HALL, C. 1905. Built in 1905, by D.H. Burnham & Co., at 220 South Michigan, this hall was not the first home of the Chicago Symphony Orchestra. Theodore Thomas, the orchestra's founder and first musical director, conducted the orchestra at the Auditorium Theatre. Unhappy with the size of the Auditorium Theatre, he worked diligently to find a new home for the orchestra; unfortunately, he died just three weeks after the new hall was dedicated in 1905. Frederick Stock was then named the new director. (Postcards Private Collection.)

THEODORE THOMAS
FOUNDER OF THE ORCHES
OCT. 11, 1835 -- JAN. 4, 19

FREDERICK STOCK
PRESENT CONDUCTOR

SYMPHONY CENTER, 2002. Previously known as Orchestra Hall, the building was renamed Symphony Center in 1995 with the addition of a new lobby Rotunda and Rehearsal Center and a six-story education center. Up until 1996, the Cliff Dwellers Club held their meetings on the top floor. The Palmer House Stables at 216 South Michigan Avenue formerly occupied part of this site. (Photo by Heather Olivia Belcher.)

CHICAGO TEMPLE, C. 1923. The Chicago Temple, located at 77 West Washington, is the home of the First United Methodist Church of Chicago. Built in 1923 by Holabird & Roche on the southeast corner of Washington and Clark, this 21-story limestone structure has the only church spire in the Loop. According to the *Guinness Book of World Records*, it is the world's tallest church at 568 feet in height. Below the 8-story steeple is the Chapel in the Sky, an octagonal chapel. This is the fifth Methodist church built on this site, with the first one dating back to 1845. (Postcard Private Collection.)

CHICAGO TEMPLE, 69 WEST WASHINGTON, THREE FIRST NATIONAL PLAZA, 2002. The Chicago Temple is now neighbored on the left by the 69 West Washington Building, formerly known as the Brunswick building, built in 1965. The Kendall, Chicago Title & Trust, Chicago Real Estate Exchange, and Stoner's Restaurant were previously built on this site. The Three First National Plaza building stands south at 70 West Madison on the northeast corner of Clark and Madison. Built in 1982 by Skidmore, Owings & Merrill, the building has two sections, one 11 stories and the other 57 stories high. The Ottawa, Harding Hotel, and Grant Hotel previously were built on this site. (Photo by Heather Olivia Belcher.)

ADLER PLANETARIUM, C. 1933 & 2002. Located at Roosevelt Road at Lake Michigan, the Adler Planetarium opened on May 12, 1930. Construction of the planetarium dates back to Burnham's Plan of Chicago in 1909. Erected on the north end of Northerly Island, the 12-sided building was designed by Ernest A. Grunsfield Jr. The planetarium was the first to be built in America, supported by a donation from Chicago philanthropist Max Adler. Lohan Associates constructed an addition, which became the new entrance, in 1981. This area was part of the site of the Century of Progress, Chicago's World's Fair of 1933-34. (Postcard Private Collection, Photo by Heather Olivia Belcher.)

X-167   TERRAZO PROMENADE AND ADLER PLANETARIUM   PRINTED IN U.S.A.

61

CHICAGO PUBLIC LIBRARY, c. 1915. This 4-story building served as Chicago's main library from 1897 until 1991. Shepley, Rutan & Coolidge constructed the building on the site of the Dearborn Park, located at 78 East Washington Street. Chicago's free library system began as a consequence of the 1871 fire when most books were destroyed. After the fire, eight thousand books were donated by England, an act Queen Victoria called the "English book donation." On January 1, 1873, the library opened in an abandoned, iron, water tank located at LaSalle and Adams Streets. On May 1, 1874, the library's circulation service was initiated. Until a permanent location was found, the library had several homes including the fourth floor of City Hall. Although the library planned to open in time for the 1893 World's Columbian Exposition, due to a lack of financial support and legal problems, the library opened on October 11, 1897. (Postcard Private Collection.)

CHICAGO CULTURAL CENTER, HAROLD WASHINGTON LIBRARY CENTER, 2002. Built in 1991, at 400 South State, the $195 million Harold Washington Library Center (right) opened on October 7, 1991. It is named after Chicago's first African-American

mayor, Harold Washington. Washington served one term as mayor (1983-1987) and died in his second term. The 10-story library center comprises 756,640 square feet, 70 miles of shelving, has over 9 million books and documents, and serves over 6,000 patrons per day. The former public library was renamed the Chicago Cultural Center, known as the "People's Palace," and was renovated in 1977 to provide free arts and cultural services. (Photos by Heather Olivia Belcher.)

CIVIC OPERA BUILDING, 1937 & 2001, OPERA HOUSE AD—1945. Located at 20 N. Wacker Drive, built in 1929 by Graham, Anderson, Probst & White, the 45-story structure is "shaped like a throne" and is home to the Chicago Lyric Opera and the Civic Theater. The building is also used for offices. The building was also known as the Kemper Insurance building. Previous to its construction, the Electric Central Manufacturing Block, and the Central Union Block stood on this site. (1937 Photo Courtesy of the University of Illinois at Chicago, 1945 Ad Courtesy of Stagebill, 2001 Photo by Heather Olivia Belcher.)

COLISEUM, 1908 AND PARKING LOT, 2002.

The postcard view, taken between June 16–19, 1908 and postmarked July 31, 1908, shows the site of the Republican National Convention held in Chicago at the Coliseum. Theodore Roosevelt, 26th President (1858–1919), had decided not to run for a third term, and supported his Secretary of War, William Howard Taft (1857–1930) to seek the nomination. Taft was successful in his run to become the 27th (one-term) President.

For the next Presidential election, the Republican Convention was again held at the Coliseum in 1912; however, Theodore Roosevelt felt that Taft had betrayed him, so he again decided to seek election, causing a split in the party. Taft won the nomination, but lost the election to Democrat Woodrow Wilson.

The Coliseum actually got its start in another state. In 1888, Charles F. Gunther, a confectioner and an avid collector of Civil War memorabilia, purchased and relocated Libby Prison, once used to house Union soldiers during the Civil War, to the area around 14th Place and South Wabash Avenue. By 1900, the prison was demolished and the Coliseum was built by architects Frost & Granger. The Coliseum, with a capacity to hold 14,000 people, was used for political conventions, sporting and other public events, until it was demolished in 1983. Today, the site is a parking lot. (Postcard Private Collection, Photo by Heather Olivia Belcher.)

**STATE AND ADAMS, PALMER HOUSE,
C. 1940, 2002. PALMER HOUSE
EMPIRE ROOM AD, 1949.** At the
northeast corner of State and Adams
stood the Leader Building, built in 1873.
The building has since been demolished
and replaced by the Unicom Thermal
Technologies Building. Immediately
behind the Leader is the Gibbs Building,
built in 1874. South on State at Monroe
stands the fourth Palmer House Hilton
Hotel, built between 1925–27. (1940
Photo Courtesy of the University of
Illinois at Chicago, 1949 Empire Room
Ad Courtesy of Stagebill, 2002 Photo by
Heather Olivia Belcher.)

BAY STATE BUILDING, ROOSEVELT THEATER—SW CORNER RANDOLPH AND STATE, 1945; BLOCK "37" 2002. In 1945, *A Bell for Adano,* starring Gene Tierney, John Hodiak, and William Bendix, was playing at the Roosevelt Theater. The Bay Building, including offices and stores, was built in 1873, and in 1887, remodeled to include the Kranz Building, by Adler and Sullivan. Kranz's, located at 126–32 State Street, next to the Roosevelt Theater, was an elegant Victorian confectionery store loved by Chicagoans until its closing in 1947. Today, the entire block (known as Block "37") is empty as shown to the right. (1945 Photo Courtesy of the University of Illinois at Chicago, 2002 Photo by Heather Olivia Belcher.)

PALMER HOUSE GRAND DINING ROOM, C. 1909. The postcard view of the Palmer House's Grand Dining Room is postmarked April 29, 1909. This view was taken in the second Palmer House, built four years after the 1871 Chicago Fire and was demolished in 1925. From the specially made table linens, marble floors, Corinthian columns, and frescoes by Italian artists, patrons were truly given a dining experience. This elegant restaurant was the site of a famous banquet in 1879, held for former President Ulysses S. Grant with Mark Twain as the dinner speaker. Grant was well-noted as a military leader during the Civil War, and as President, he tried to mend the wounds of the war by bringing together the north and south. However, most businesses he tried failed, and he had many financial problems. In order to support his family, he began writing short stories. He arranged for his friend, Mark Twain, to publish his wartime memoirs. The book was considered a bestseller. Over the years, there have been a variety of dining choices available in the Loop, and it continues to be an area where there is something for everyone. (Postcard Private Collection.)

Chapter 5
ENJOYABLE FINE DINING

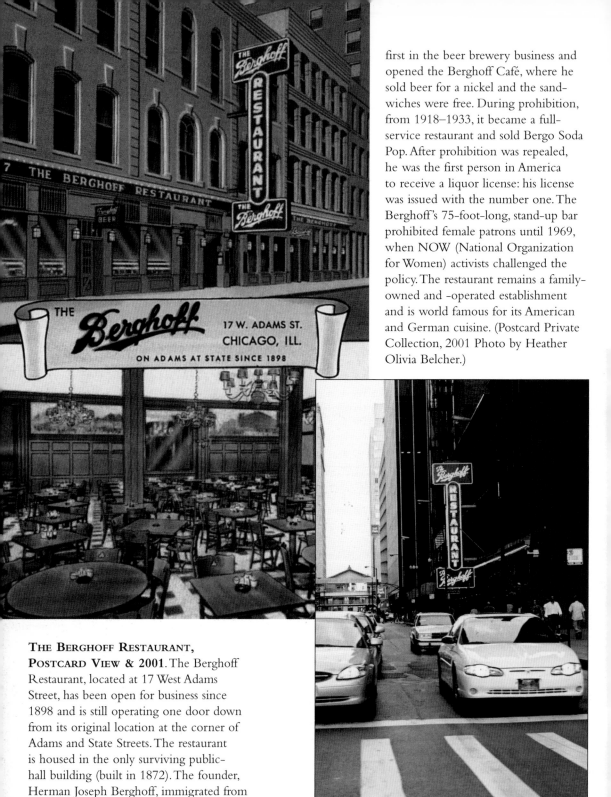

first in the beer brewery business and opened the Berghoff Café, where he sold beer for a nickel and the sandwiches were free. During prohibition, from 1918–1933, it became a full-service restaurant and sold Bergo Soda Pop. After prohibition was repealed, he was the first person in America to receive a liquor license: his license was issued with the number one. The Berghoff's 75-foot-long, stand-up bar prohibited female patrons until 1969, when NOW (National Organization for Women) activists challenged the policy. The restaurant remains a family-owned and -operated establishment and is world famous for its American and German cuisine. (Postcard Private Collection, 2001 Photo by Heather Olivia Belcher.)

THE BERGHOFF RESTAURANT, POSTCARD VIEW & 2001. The Berghoff Restaurant, located at 17 West Adams Street, has been open for business since 1898 and is still operating one door down from its original location at the corner of Adams and State Streets. The restaurant is housed in the only surviving public-hall building (built in 1872). The founder, Herman Joseph Berghoff, immigrated from Dortsmund, Germany in 1870. He was

FORUM CAFETERIA AND OTHER WEST MADISON STREET BUSINESSES, C. 1960, THREE FIRST NATIONAL PLAZA BUILDING LOBBY, 2002. Next to Tad's Steak House and the Today Theater, the Forum Cafeteria offered affordable dining options in the Loop area. This block formerly included the Harding Hotel (once known as the Planter's Hotel), Ottawa Building, and the Grant Hotel. In 1982, Three First National Plaza Building was built from the northwest corner of Dearborn to the northeast corner of Clark along Madison Street. The building is a combination 11-story and 57-story building with multiple sections, designed by Skidmore, Owings & Merrill. (1960 Photo Courtesy of the University of Illinois at Chicago, 2002 Photo by Heather Olivia Belcher.)

chocolate sodas, coal candy made out of licorice and shaped like coal briquettes, sugar teddy bears, and chocolate mice. After Mr. Kranz's death in 1919, his daughter, Florence Kranz, continued the business. Miss Kranz was known for her unique selection of chocolates known as the Florentine chocolates, named after her. The business closed in 1947. Today, this block is a vacant lot, known as "Block 37." There have been discussions over the years to develop this area into a major retail complex or a park area. (Kranz Photo Courtesy of the University of Illinois at Chicago, Block "37" Photo by Heather Olivia Belcher.)

KRANZ'S CONFECTIONERY STORE, BLOCK "37," 2002. Gone, but not forgotten. The Kranz's Confectionery Store began in 1868 on Blue Island Avenue by John Kranz, who immigrated to America from Germany at the age of 15. In 1881, the Kranz Store moved to 126–30 State Street and very little changed until the building was remodeled in the 1890s, and electric fixtures replaced the gaslights. Although no food was served except for pastries, ice cream, candies, and beverages, Mr. Kranz's fame continued over the years as he introduced the very latest creations from Europe made by highly specialized candy artists. Many of his creations were world renowned, such as his

HENRICI'S RESTAURANT, C. 1951 & 2002, RICHARD J. DALEY CIVIC CENTER, 2002. Henrici's, founded by Phillip Henrici in 1868, was originally located in "Newspaper Row" near Madison and Wells Streets. In 1893, the German Bakery/Restaurant, moved to 67–71 West Randolph Street in Chicago's Theater District. Holsman & Hunt designed the 6-story building. Phillip Henrici was from an old Vienna family of famous restaurateurs. The walls of the restaurant were decorated with oil paintings that Henrici had collected from around the world. The restaurant was dedicated to the fine art of dining. Lillian Russell, Ellen Terry, and other stars who appeared in the nearby theaters, were regular guests. In 1929, the J.R. Thompson chain bought out the restaurant. Henrici's closed in August 1962, and was

HENRICI'S
67 W. RANDOLPH ST.

Tear Drop .06	Sparkling Water .02
Citrate .04	Quinac .02 (Thimbles)

LOW CALORIE DIET

MONDAY
Breakfast: Weak Tea
Lunch: One Bouillon Cube in One-half Cup Diluted Water
Dinner: One Pigeon Thigh; Three Ounces Prune Juice (gargle only)

TUESDAY
Breakfast: Scraped Crumbs from Burnt Toast
Lunch: One Doughnut Hole (without sugar), One Glass of Dehydrated Water
Dinner: Three grains cornmeal, broiled

WEDNESDAY
Breakfast: Shredded Egg Shell Skin
Lunch: One-half Dozen Poppy Seeds
Dinner: Bee's Knees and Mosquito Knuckles Sauted in Vinegar

THURSDAY
Breakfast: Boiled-Out Stains of Old Table Cloth
Lunch: Belly Button of a Naval Orange
Dinner: Three Eyes from Irish Potato (diced)

FRIDAY
Breakfast: Two Lobster Antennas
Lunch: One Tail Joint of Sea Horse
Dinner: Rotisserie Broiled Guppy Fillet

SATURDAY
Breakfast: Four Chopped Banana Seeds
Lunch: Broiled Butterfly Liver
Dinner: Jelly Vertebrae a la Centipede

SUNDAY
Breakfast: Pickled Humming Bird Tongue
Lunch: Prime Rib of Tadpole; Aroma of Empty Custard Pie Plate
Dinner: Tossed Paprika and Clover Leaf Salad

NOTE: A seven-ounce glass of steam may be consumed on alternate days to help in having something to blow off.

eventually demolished due to the building of the Richard J. Daley Civic Center, named after the 39th mayor of Chicago. The postcard above shows a light-hearted way to lose weight! (Postcards Private Collection, 2002 Photo by Heather Olivia Belcher.)

71

Eitel RESTAURANT

"Famous for Good Food"

Luncheons from 45c
In Main Dining Room from 55c
Dinner $1.50

Heidelberg Octet

Harriet O'Rourke,
Soloist

★

Downstairs:
Louie and His Gang

★

Afternoon Tea 3:00 to 5:00 daily
55c up

Wednesday, lectures at 3:30 P.M.

RANDOLPH Just West of **STATE**

West Randolph, near the northeast corner of Randolph and State Streets. The spacious restaurant specialized in Czechoslovakian and German food. On March 26, 2002, after a $2.5 million renovation project to convert this once restaurant into a three-theater complex, the Nobel Fool Theater opened. This 8,000 square-foot complex will specialize in comedic productions, improvisations, cabaret shows, a bar, and a comedy school. The previous tenant at this location was Ronnie's Steak Palace. (Postcard Private Collection, Ad Courtesy Stagebill, Photo by Heather Olivia Belcher.)

EITEL'S OLD HEIDELBERG, C. 1948 & 2002, AD, 1937. Graham, Anderson, Probst & White built Robert and Max Eitel's Old Heidelberg Restaurant in 1934, located at 16

WACKER DRIVE AND SKYLINE ON CHICAGO RIVER, C. 1930. This photograph, taken in the 1930s, shows the various transportation options available to Loop visitors and workers. The Chicago River continues to be a busy water access way for commercial and pleasure boats, allowing access to the Great Lakes and other ports around the world. The bridges provide access from the Loop across the river to the north side of the city. There are 20 bridges in the downtown Loop area. Before 1832, when the first bridge was built, the only way to get across the river was by boat. The Wells Street Bridge, shown below, provides this access to elevated trains and vehicles. The bi-level Wacker Drive, built in the mid–1920s, replaced the South Water Produce Market. (Photo Courtesy of the University of Illinois at Chicago.)

Chapter 6

VIEWS AROUND THE LOOP

Wacker Drive and Sky Line on Chicago River

On STATE ST., CHICAGO.

planking, macadam, wooden blocks, and later cobblestones. The concrete streets used in the modern era will sometimes expose the old cobblestones it covers. The J.B. Wilson Studio portrait of the young man was probably taken around the turn of the 20th century. The studio was located at 389 State Street. (Postcard & Portrait Photo Private Collection, Photo by Heather Olivia Belcher.)

LOOP ATTIRE/LOOP STREETS, C. 1900 & 2002, J.B. WILSON STUDIO PORTRAIT, DATE UNKNOWN. The "dress code" for those in the Loop has relaxed somewhat over the past century. Women no longer wear hoped skirts, hats, and gloves, and men no longer wear derby hats. Attire today is more varied and tends to be more casual. On the postcard view, postmarked September 27, 1900, and mailed to Germany, note the cobblestones used along State Street. The streets of early Chicago were muddy. Women's long skirts were often muddy and soiled. By 1858, Chicago had raised itself out of the mud. Early pavement of streets consisted of wooden

MERCHANDISE MART, C. 1930 & 2001.
The Merchandise Mart, located east of
Wolf Point, where the three branches of
the Chicago River converge, is the world's
largest commercial building with 60% of
the building used for wholesale design
showrooms. The address is 200 World
Trade Center, and it is so large that it has
its own zip code: 60654. It was designed
by the firm of Graham, Anderson, Probst,
and White and built by Marshall Field's
and Company during the depression in
1929, with the grand-opening on May 5,
1930. The Mart has been renovated and
remodeled several times. James Simpson,
president of Marshall Field's from 1923
to 1930 and chairman of the Chicago Plan
Commission from 1926 to 1935, selected
the site. The impressive structure has 4.2
million square feet, is two blocks long,
and has 25 stories. The Mart was built on
the site that was formerly occupied by
the Chicago & Northwestern Railway
Wells Street Terminal, built in 1882 and
demolished in 1927.

In 1945, Joseph P. Kennedy, father of
President John F. Kennedy, purchased the
property. The Merchants Hall of Fame,
a brainchild of Kennedy, was started in
1935 to honor American merchants. Eight
bronze busts mounted in front of the
Mart represent those inducted into the
Hall of Fame. The Mart has been owned
and managed by the Kennedy family for
over 50 years. (Postcard Private Collection,
Photo by Heather Olivia Belcher.)

Merchandise Mart

over 134 routes and 1,937 route miles. Private tour bus companies are also in operation, some are designed to look like the trolley cable cars of the past. (Postcard Private Collection, Photos by Heather Olivia Belcher.)

PUBLIC TRANSPORTATION—BUS LINES, c. 1917, 2002. During the late-19th century and early-20th century, Chicagoans had to rely on public transportation, as horse and buggy ownership was too costly for most working-class citizens. Horse-drawn omnibuses, such as the Franklin Parmalee, began service in 1853, most often over muddy Chicago streets. Horse-drawn streetcars also offered another form of public transportation. The first horse-drawn rail streetcar traveled down State Street from Randolph to Twelfth Street on February 14, 1859. Cable cars began appearing in 1882. In 1917, the Autobus operated by the Chicago Motor Bus Company, had a number of double-decker buses that operated on those streets that did not offer rail transit services from the Loop to north side locations. The Chicago Transit Authority (CTA) began operation on October 1, 1947, after acquiring the Chicago Rapid Transit Company and private Chicago Surface Lines. On October 1, 1952, the CTA purchased the Chicago Motor Coach System and become the only operator of Chicago transit operations. Today, the CTA has approximately 1,900 buses, operating

Eastland Disaster, 1915, Goodrich Line Steamboats, c. 1908, Chicago River at Clark Street Bridge, 2002. On the morning of July 24, 1915, Chicago witnessed one of the darkest events in its history. Western Electric employees, families, and friends boarded the steamer Eastland on its way to their annual company picnic in Michigan City, Indiana. The Eastland was moored to her dock between Clark and LaSalle Streets on the south bank of the Chicago River. At 7:28 a.m. as the ship left the dock, the ship capsized. Of the 2,572 people on board, 844 lost their lives. Apparently, recent modifications (additional lifeboats), made the ship unstable. Approximately 22 entire families were lost. Over the next 20 years, many lawsuits were filed, however there were no rulings that the ship owners were responsible for the deaths. The Eastland was renamed the *U.S.S. Wilmette* and was refitted to be a naval training ship. In 1947, the ship was broken up for scrap materials. The postcard view, *c.*1908, of the Goodrich Docks is near the Eastland disaster that would occur four years later.

SCENE OF ·EASTLAND DISAST 8 A.M. JULY-24-1915

The Clark Street Bridge at the south bank of the Chicago River looking west. Wacker Drive, is at the time of this writing, closed due to a renovation project, but the Clark Street Bridge remains open. The building along the bank has changed the skyline view of the Loop from the northern side of the Loop. The Chicago River continues to be used both for boating pleasure and commercial access. (Postcards Private Collection, Photo by Heather Olivia Belcher.)

VIEW FROM STATE STREET BRIDGE, C. 1928, 2001. Across the Chicago River, looking south is the northern view of the Loop area. The newly completed Wacker Drive served as a transportation marvel to Loop traffic as well as parking facilities on both the upper and lower levels. From the varied styles of the London Guarantee & Accident Building to the Pure Oil Building along Wacker Drive, it is a testament to the early-20th century architects today. The "Revive Wacker Drive" project is ongoing and scheduled for completion in November 2002. (1928 Photo Courtesy of the University of Illinois at Chicago, 2001 Photo by Heather Olivia Belcher.)

WACKER DRIVE CONSTRUCTION c. 1926, RECONSTRUCTION 2002. The bi-level Charles H. Wacker Drive, built on the Chicago River's edge and based on Daniel Burnham's 1909 Plan of Chicago, replaced the old South Water Street Market. The drive was named for Charles H. Wacker (1856-1929), first chairman of the Chicago Plan Commission, a civic leader, brewery owner, and biggest supporter of the plan. Wacker used innovative marketing methods to the citizens of Chicago to gain massive support of the plan. The original plan used the upper level for local traffic and pedestrian walkways, and the lower level for heavy commercial traffic. Construction took place between 1926 and 1928, and construction costs were around $8 million. Built by Edward H. Bennett, assistant to Burnham, the design followed Burnham's plan that included a beltway around the Loop. However, only the drive on the north section was completed. The plan for the southern east-west section was never realized. The $200 million "Revive Wacker Drive" project to repair the aging drive began in February 2001 and is scheduled for completion by November 2002. Sections of the drive are closed during the renovation and unfortunately businesses along the closed sections have been impacted by loss of revenue. (1926 Photo Courtesy of the University of Illinois at Chicago, 2002 Photo by Heather Olivia Belcher.)

skyscraper," it was built on a 65-by-10- foot lot in 1928. On the right is the 17-story Chicago Club, built in 1928 by Holabird & Roche. This building located at 68 East Wacker was renamed the Wacker Tower Office Center and a conversion condo is in progress. In the good-old days, parking was plentiful on upper and lower Wacker Drive. Today, the view below contains the above buildings, with a few new neighbors. On the left is One Illinois Center, built in 1971 and the Clarion Executive Plaza Hotel, built in 1960. On the far right is the Pure Oil building built in 1926 by Giaver & Dinkelberg, with Thielbar & Fugard. The 24-story building with a 17-story tower was formerly known as the Jewelers building, later renamed American Life Insurance building and later the 35 East Wacker Drive building. Formerly on this site stood the 1872 Standard Oil Building. (1929 Photo Courtesy of the University of Illinois at Chicago, 2001 Photo by Heather Olivia Belcher.)

NORTH VIEW OF LOOP/WACKER DRIVE, 1929 & 2001. The above view of the northern Loop includes the following buildings: 333 North Michigan Avenue (35-story), built in 1928 by Holabird & Roche; London Guarantee & Accident (21-story, also known as Stone Container and later renamed the 360 North Michigan Avenue Building), 1923, A.S. Alschuler; Mather Tower (24-story, also known as the Lincoln Tower and now as the 75 East Wacker Building), 1928, Herbert H. Riddle. The Mather Tower, built with an 18-story tower, was called "Chicago's skinniest

DELAWARE BUILDING, C. 1915, 2002.
Wheelock and Thomas built one of the few surviving structures from the post-Chicago Fire development, the landmark Delaware, in 1874. Located at 36 West Randolph, on the northeast corner of Randolph and Dearborn Streets, the 8-story building was originally built as 6-stories. Julius H. Huber made a 2-story addition in 1888. Wilbert R. Hasbrouck renovated the Italianate-style building in 1982. The building was also known as the Real Estate Board Building and Bryant Building. In the postcard view below, the building is located immediately west of the Iroquois (Colonial) Theatre, the site of a disastrous fire that occurred on December 30, 1903, resulting in the loss of 602 lives, including many children. In the photograph at right, McDonald's restaurant occupies the first two floors of the building. (Postcard Private Collection, Photo by Heather Olivia Belcher.)

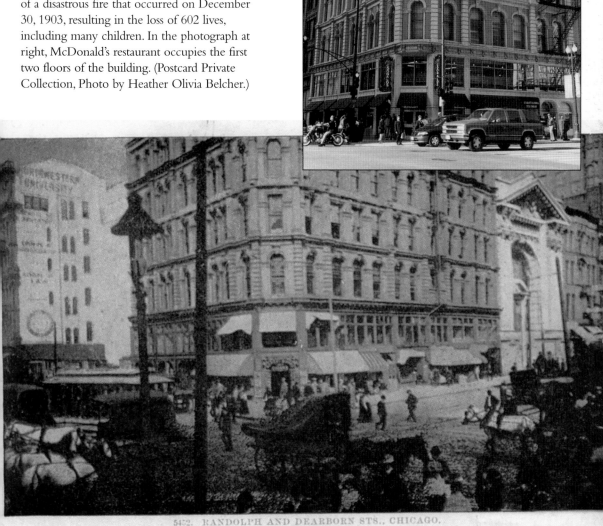

5452. RANDOLPH AND DEARBORN STS., CHICAGO.

Chicago's mayoral history has been an interesting one, starting with the first mayor, William B. Ogden, elected on May 2, 1837, he served 1837–38. The first African-American mayor, the 42nd mayor, Harold Washington, was elected for two terms, the first one in 1983–87. He died in office during his second term on November 25, 1987. The main Chicago Library Center is named after Washington. The shortest-term mayor, David Orr, served as acting mayor after Harold Washington's death, from November 25 to December 2, 1987. The first female mayor, the 41st mayor, Jane Byrne, was elected and served one term in 1979-83. Richard J. Daley, the 39th and longest-term mayor is also the father of the current mayor. He was elected to six terms and served between 1955-76. He died on December 20, 1976. The current mayor, 45th mayor, Richard M. Daley, is approaching his father's record, having been elected to 4 terms, 1989 to the present. Prior to 1907, mayors served 2-year terms, but after that year, mayoral terms were changed to 4-year terms. (Postcard private collection, 1928 Photo Courtesy of the University of Illinois at Chicago, 2002 Photo by Heather Olivia Belcher.)

City Hall, Chicago, Ill.

CITY HALL/COOK COUNTY BUILDING, C. 1885, 1928 & 2002. The postcard view shows the second City Hall/Cook County Building, which was completed in 1885, by architects James Egan and Alex Kirkland. Open trolley cars are seen in the photograph. This structure was demolished in 1909 to make room for the current structure. The postcard was mailed on December 10, 1907. The third and current 12-story City Hall/County Building was completed in 1911 by Holabird & Roche. The first City Hall, which included the County Courthouse, was also constructed on this location by John Osdel in 1853, but was destroyed by the Chicago Fire of 1871.

CHICAGO POST OFFICE, c. 1933. The post office at right was dedicated on February 15, 1933, and was built at the cost $22 million by Graham, Anderson, Probst & White. The postal facility was built in proximity to Union Station, at 433 West Van Buren, to facilitate the transfer of mail quickly. The structure is built over the air rights to the railroad tracks leading to Union Station and extends from Harrison to Van Buren, from Canal Street to the Chicago River. At the time it was built, it was considered the largest and most technically equipped Post Office in the world. The

161—New Post Office, Chicago

flat roof was designed as an airplane landing field. This post office facility, which the Eisenhower Expressway runs directly through, is vacant at this time. There have been several locations of the Chicago Post Office. (Postcard Private Collection.)

VACANT CHICAGO POST OFFICE, 2002. AND GENERAL MAIL FACILITY, 2002. The new post office, pictured in the bottom right photo, is a new state-of-the-art facility, built in 1996 at 433 West Harrison Street. Built by Lester B. Knight, at the corner of Canal and Polk Streets, the 8-story construction has one million square feet of space. (Photos by Heather Olivia Belcher.)

but allowances were made to add 16 stories. Daniel Burnham was initially hired to design the station, but died before the designs were completed. Estimates are that the station cost between $50 and $75 million. The name "Union" came from the union of four railroads that originally used the depot's facilities: the Chicago, Burlington & Quincy, the Chicago & Alton, the Chicago, Milwaukee & St. Paul, and the Pennsylvania Railroad. The station went through significant renovations in 1994–1995 and continues to be a transportation center for the city of Chicago and the country. (Postcards Private Collection, Photo by Heather Olivia Belcher.)

UNION DEPOT, C. 1910, UNION STATION, C.1924 & 2002. The first Union Depot was erected in 1881, on the northeast corner of Canal and Adams. The 4-story structure was designed by W.W. Boyington and demolished in 1923. The 120 Riverside Plaza Building now occupies this site. Adjacent to this site, the current Union Station, at 210 South Canal, was completed in 1924 by Graham, Burnham & Co. The designs were for a 5-story building,

**CHICAGO DAILY NEWS BUILDING,
c.1930, 2 NORTH RIVERSIDE PLAZA,
2001.** The Chicago Daily News Building, located at 400 West Madison Street, occupies a full block. Completed in 1929, by Holabird & Roche, it was the first Chicago building to be constructed on railroad air rights. The building served as home to the *Chicago Daily News* newspaper that started on January 2, 1876, at 15 North Wells Street. The paper was purchased by Marshall Field in 1959 and was discontinued on March 4, 1978. It was the last newspaper in Chicago to be published only in the afternoon. Mike Royko and Carl Sandburg are some of the world-renowned writers once employed by the *Daily News*. Today, the building has been renamed 2 North Riverside Plaza and continues to be a retail and office building, in addition to providing access to the Metra trains of Northwestern Station. (1930 Photo Courtesy of the University of Illinois at Chicago, 2001 Photo by Heather Olivia Belcher.)

the height of the Prudential Building. (1959 Photo Courtesy of the University of Illinois at Chicago, 2001 Photo by Heather Olivia Belcher.)

PRUDENTIAL BUILDING AND NEIGHBORS, 1959 & 2001. The Prudential Building, now known as One Prudential Plaza, when built in 1955 was the city's tallest skyscraper, rising 42 stories over the air rights of the Illinois Central Railroad yards. The architects were Naess & Murphy. This was the first major building built since the Depression. In the foreground stands the Monroe Street Parking lot that is now being replaced by Millennium Park. Today, there are a number of buildings in the area that have surpassed

ART INSTITUTE LIONS WATCH OVER MICHIGAN AVENUE, 1929 & 2002. From the far left at Adams Street, going north, the following buildings are pictured: People's Gas (1911), Municipal Court/Lakeview (1906), Illinois Athletic Club (1908), Monroe (1912), University Club (1909), Gage Building Group–Gage, Keith, & Ascher (1898), Chicago Athletic Club (1893), Willoughby Tower (1929), Montgomery Ward Tower (1899), 14 North Michigan/Ward (1885), People's Trust & Savings Bank/Michigan Boulevard (1914), Chicago Public Library (1897), John Crerar Library (1920), and Carbide & Carbon (1929). Most of the buildings are still standing today and are virtually unchanged, except for a few. Also, parking is no longer allowed on this stretch of Michigan Avenue. (1929 Photo Courtesy of the University of Illinois at Chicago, 2002 Photo by Heather Olivia Belcher.)

so popular, he got out of the soap business and focused his attention on gum. Not far from the Wrigley Building is Pioneer Court, which marks the homestead location of Chicago's first settler, businessman and Catholic, Jean Baptiste Point du Sable (1745-1818). DuSable, a fur trader and a Black French-speaking native of Saint-Domingue, came to Chicago in 1779. He set up a trading post on the north bank of the Chicago River and lived with his wife, Catherine, a Pottawatomi Indian, and their children.

At night, high-intensity floodlights illuminate the cream-colored terra-cotta building, which makes the Wrigley Building sparkle and it has become a symbol of Chicago. (Postcard Private Collection, Photo by Heather Olivia Belcher.)

WRIGLEY BUILDING, 1933 & 2001. The Wrigley Building was the city's first building to have air-conditioning. Built in two phases, the south section, built in 1921, is 17-stories tall and includes an 11-story tower, and is located at the southwest corner of Michigan and North Water Street. The north section, built in 1924, is 19-stories, and is located on the southwest corner of North Michigan and Hubbard Street. The architects Graham, Anderson, Probst & White designed both sections of the building. The chewing gum magnate, William K. Wrigley Jr., who first got his start in the soap business, commissioned the building. He included chewing gum in each box of soap, but the gum got

THE MICHIGAN AVENUE BRIDGE. Edward H. Bennett, from 1918 to 1920, needed to design an improved bridge over the swing-type used in the Rush Street Bridge. The Michigan Avenue Bridge was constructed to solve the many transportation problems, both in the Chicago River and on land. It was the world's first double-leaf, double-deck, trunnion bascule bridge, having the ability to handle two levels of traffic and open and close in under 60 seconds. Four limestone bridge houses trace the bridge at each end, although only the northwest house is in use. (Postcards Private Collection, Photo by Heather Olivia Belcher.)

RUSH STREET BRIDGE, C. 1900, VIEW FROM MICHIGAN AVENUE BRIDGE, C. 1930, 2002. The first Rush Street Bridge was built in 1856 at the cost of $48,000. Over the years, due to various mishaps, the bridge was replaced. On September 19, 1856, a boat at the Lake House Ferry capsized from crossing the Chicago River, near the iron bridge. On board were mostly laborers, all men, on their way to work. On November 3, 1863, a herd of cattle crossing the bridge caused it to collapse, resulting in the loss of men and cattle. The Chicago Fire of 1871 destroyed the rebuilt bridge. In 1920, upon completion of the Michigan Avenue Bridge, the Rush Street Bridge was finally removed. The postcard view of the Rush Street Bridge around the turn of the century shows the Goodrich Docks, various warehouses and other docks along the congested Chicago River.

MONADNOCK BUILDING c. 1915 & 2002. Four sections, named after New England Mountains, comprise the landmark Monadnock. The northern half of the building, located at 53 West Jackson, was built by Burnham & Root in 1891, and was named Monadnock and Kearsage (mountains in New Hampshire). The southern half, located at 54 West Van Buren, was built by Holabird & Roche in 1893, and was named Wachusetts (Massachusetts) and Katahdin (Maine). Over the years, only the Monadnock name remained. Monadnock is a geological term that means a granite mountain surrounded by a glacial plain. It was considered to be the world's tallest stone building at that time. Today, as in the past, the building continues to provide office space for retail and commercial customers. (Postcard Private collection, Photos by Heather Olivia Belcher.)

TACOMA BUILDING, 1918 & ONE NORTH LaSALLE BUILDING, 2002. Holabird & Roche built the Tacoma Building, located on the northeast corner of LaSalle and Madison, in 1888 at a cost of $500,000. It was home to lawyers, real estate offices, and insurance agencies. On May 12, 1929, the 12-story building was demolished. This site was previously occupied by the Schweizer Block (1872–1888). The Tacoma was replaced by the 49-story One North LaSalle Street Building built in 1930 by architects, Vitzhum & Burns and is currently going through some renovation. (1918 Photo Courtesy of the University of Illinois at Chicago, 2002 Photo by Heather Olivia Belcher.)

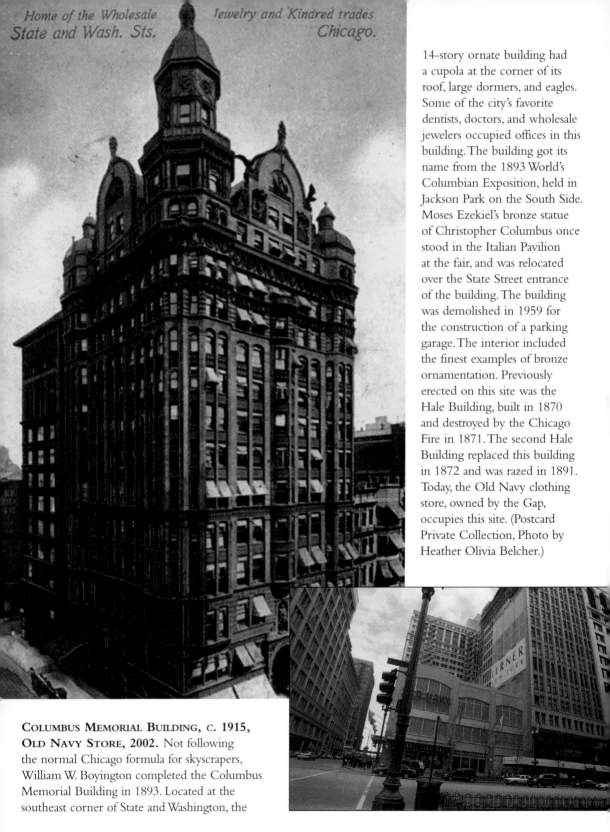

14-story ornate building had a cupola at the corner of its roof, large dormers, and eagles. Some of the city's favorite dentists, doctors, and wholesale jewelers occupied offices in this building. The building got its name from the 1893 World's Columbian Exposition, held in Jackson Park on the South Side. Moses Ezekiel's bronze statue of Christopher Columbus once stood in the Italian Pavilion at the fair, and was relocated over the State Street entrance of the building. The building was demolished in 1959 for the construction of a parking garage. The interior included the finest examples of bronze ornamentation. Previously erected on this site was the Hale Building, built in 1870 and destroyed by the Chicago Fire in 1871. The second Hale Building replaced this building in 1872 and was razed in 1891. Today, the Old Navy clothing store, owned by the Gap, occupies this site. (Postcard Private Collection, Photo by Heather Olivia Belcher.)

COLUMBUS MEMORIAL BUILDING, c. 1915, OLD NAVY STORE, 2002. Not following the normal Chicago formula for skyscrapers, William W. Boyington completed the Columbus Memorial Building in 1893. Located at the southeast corner of State and Washington, the

PULLMAN BUILDING, c. 1920, PEOPLE'S GAS, LIGHT & COKE BUILDING, c. 1920 & 2002. The 10-story building in the center of the above postcard was the headquarters for the offices of George M. Pullman, owner of the Palace Car Co. sleeping railroad cars. The Pullman Building, located at the southwest corner of Michigan and Adams at 79 East Adams was built in 1884 by Solon S. Beman. In addition to offices, it housed the luxury apartments that were home to famous Chicagoans such as Florenz Ziegfeld Jr. For many years, the Tip Top Inn, a famous Chicago restaurant with a fabulous view of the lakefront, was located on the ninth floor. Many people from the theatrical community enjoyed the food and ambiance: Lillian Russell, George M. Cohan, and Anna Held, to

name a few. The Pullman Building was razed in 1956 to make room for the Borg Warner Building, built in 1958. Across the street, at 122 South Michigan, was the headquarters for the Peoples Gas, Light & Coke Building, now called the People's Gas Company. The 20-story building pictured in the postcard and photo is actually the second building for People's Gas, built in 1911 by D.H. Burnham & Company. Previously, the first People's Gas Building was built as the Brunswick Hotel in 1883 by Burnham & Root, and destroyed in 1910. (Postcard Private Collection, Photo by Heather Olivia Belcher.)

MADISON & DEARBORN—ANDES CANDIES, COVENANT CLUB, BRUNSWICK, C. 1960, 2002. A variety of restaurants and businesses occupied this corner, including Harding's, one of several of John P. Harding's restaurants in Chicago, which was located at 68 West Madison, and Andes Candies, one of the many chains around the city. Another business, Tad's Steak House, offered a steak dinner for $1.29. The Today Theater, as well as other nearby businesses, have all been replaced by 3 First National Plaza, pictured below. Around the corner, the Covenant Club, located at 10 North Dearborn and built

in 1923 by Walter W. Ahlschlager, still exists today and has been renamed as the 10 North Dearborn Building. On the right, the Brunswick Building still exists, located at 69 West Washington and built in 1965 by Skidmore, Owings & Merrill. Cook County purchased the office building in 1996. (1960 Photo Courtesy of the University of Illinois at Chicago, Ad Courtesy Stagebill, 2002 Photo by Heather Olivia Belcher.)

WATER TOWER AND PUMPING STATION, C. 1940 & 2001. The Water Tower and Pumping Station were some of the few buildings to survive the Great Chicago Fire of 1871. Designed by W.W. Boyington and completed in 1869, the 154-foot tower was built to hide the 138-foot iron standpipe used to control the water pressure from the Pumping Station. There have been many attempts to destroy the Water Tower. In 1918, City Planners targeted the tower for demolition, but the structure was saved by then Mayor William "Big Bill" Thompson who ordered the new Michigan Avenue (once known as Pine) built around the Tower. Later, there was a proposal to tear the tower down to build an apartment complex and later an arts center. It has survived and has become the "symbol of the city's will to survive." The Palmolive Building (now the Playboy Building) with the famous Lindbergh Beacon on the top, was built in 1929. The Lindbergh Beacon operated from 1951 to 1981, but was removed because of complaints from nearby high-rise neighbors that the light shone into their windows. A new beacon was installed last year and has been tested several times, with mixed

reviews. There are still complaints about the brightness. As shown in the pictures above and right, the Water Tower and Pumping station look the same, although much has changed to the area surrounding these structures. (Postcard Private Collection, Photos by Heather Olivia Belcher.)